ALL IS WELL

OPPORTUNITIES IN PROBLEMS

ANSHUMAN SHARMA

Made with ♥ on the Notion Press Platform
www.notionpress.com

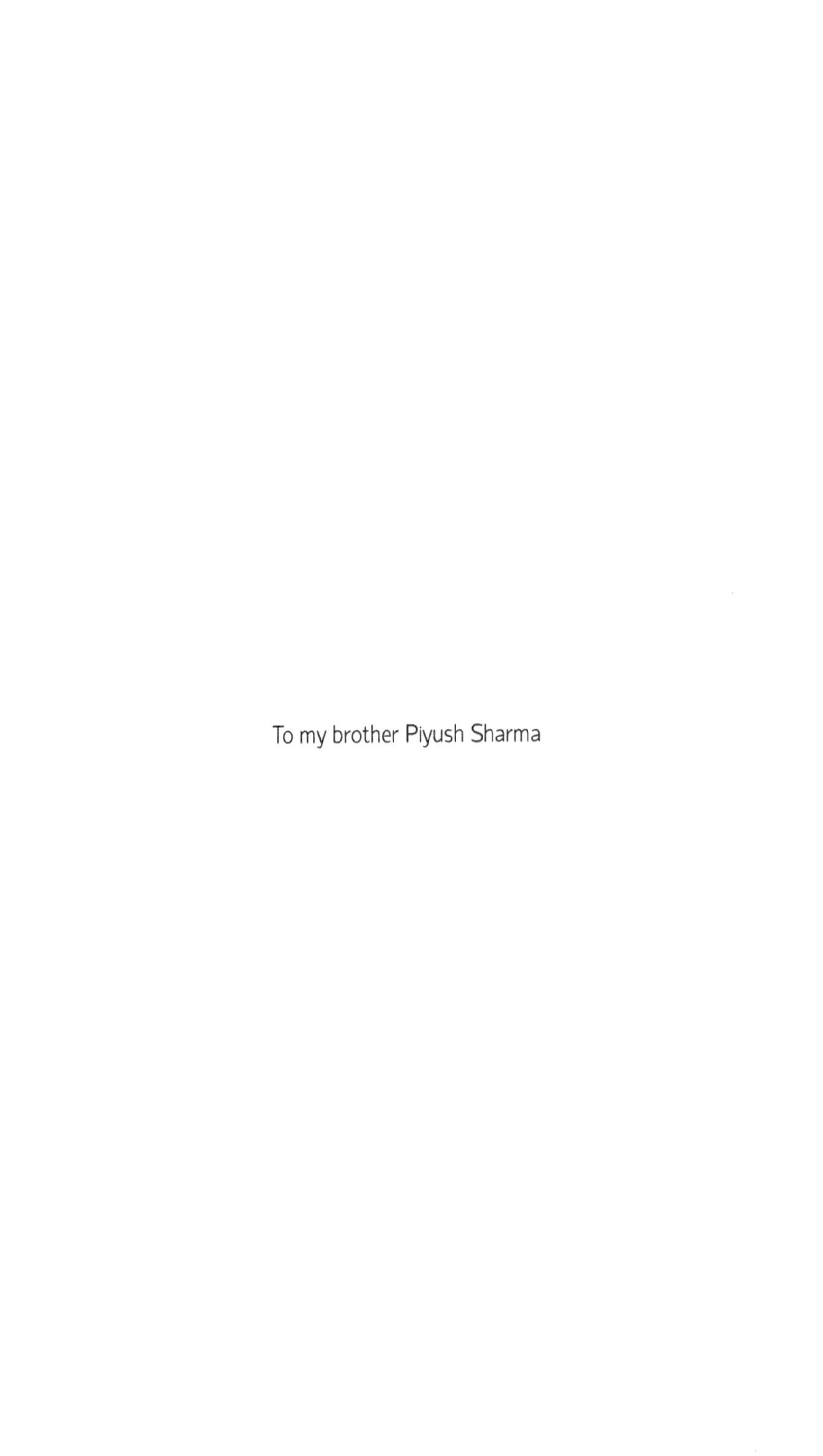

To my brother Piyush Sharma

Contents

Contents

Contents

Contents

Preface

Humans are different from animals mainly because of their ability to think. The thinking process and actions taken by individuals create the difference in the lives of two humans. An unsuccessful person claims the problems in his life as the main culprit, while a successful person would use same problems to get success and happiness in life. We see successful human beings in offices, society and markets. They are considered successful because of their achievements, money they possess, power they wield or confidence they radiate. Most people want to be like them and wish for their luck, without understanding the real difference between them and others.

The definition of success is different for every individual, some consider peace of mind as success for others money is important, some find more time with family as bliss while others want to travel. A successful life doesn't mean the life with money and power but a satisfactory, happy and positive life. A person can be unsuccessful even after having all amenities of life and being surrounded by yes men.

Researchers have done extensive analysis to find the difference between successful and unsuccessful persons. Looking at all the aspects, the only difference which could be found is the perception of happenings in life. For an unsuccessful person life is full of negativities and problems. Every event is perceived in the most negative form, which put pressure on life and body. They get stress and are unable to think straight about the problem. Even for simple problems they are not able to find solutions and take actions. Even when opportunities arrive they are not able to get the benefits of them as they are too busy with their problems.

An unsuccessful person would look at all negative aspects of events in life while a successful person would look at the same events in completely different way, he would see all positives in it, and few people may even find opportunities in it. For a successful person all happenings in life are events. All facts of the event are analyzed and understood, which are then looked in positive and empowering ways. Even the extreme negative cases are viewed positively to get least affected by them, instead learn from those events. This habit of successful and happy people makes them optimistic in life, which allows them to take the maximum advantage of the situation to get success.

This book looks at some events of life and tries to view them in optimistic ways. I interacted with a large number of successful people to look for their secrets. In most of the cases I found the similar ways of perceiving the events of their life. These events are neither good nor bad; they are just events, open to an empowering or a negative perception. What we describe here are a number of events and right way of perceiving them.

The process of rightly perceiving any event is extremely simple, which would require a consciously created optimistic thinking process. Our mind tends to look at most of the happenings of life in passive ways. We need to train our mind with right statements and questions to feel positive and in control of the situation. This book covers a number of such events followed by empowering statements and questions to focus on the positive side of each event. This diversion of attention would help you to protect yourself from any harm which the event can cause, instead use it as a learning platform to make you successful in life.

Most of you would be familiar with these events, which are generally termed as problems. You can read them, one at a time, while grasping the thinking process of successful people. You can also use them during challenging times, understand the event and find ways to perceive them, rightly.

CHAPTER ONE

Event 1 – Lost the Job

Points to Consider

1. What is my ambition or dream in life? With the present facts what is the best way to achieve it?
2. How other successful people used this event to change the course of their life? How the similar events acted like an opportunity for them?
3. How can this event be an opportunity in my life?
4. What is my learning from this event? How can I use this learning to act better in future?
5. What are my immediate targets? What actions I need to take now to get those targets?
6. What are the risks I need to be careful of and what actions I should take to protect myself from any potential problems?
7. What I need to be to get success? What actions I need to take now?

CHAPTER TWO

Event 2 – Not Able to Get a Job

Points to Consider

1. What I want in my life? How this event could help me to get my dreams?
2. What are the main areas which can help me to fulfill my ambition? How can I use them to get immediate success?
3. How other successful people used similar event in their life to move in the right direction? Am I doing right things? Is there anything missing which can help me to get success?
4. What other skills do I have which can help me to earn and build a better career?
5. What I need to be to enjoy the process? What actions I need to take now?

CHAPTER THREE

Event 3 – Harassment in Job

Points to Consider

1. Why am I accepting this harassment? Why will it continue if not stopped?
2. It is a crime to let this happen to me. It is affecting me mentally and physically, which I would never permit. How this event is taking me away from my dreams?
3. What are the risks associated with acting against it? How can I manage those risks?
4. What are the best ways to get it stopped immediately? Which method would suit my purpose?
5. What I want to be in my life? What are various other options which would help me to get there?
6. What actions I need to take immediately?

CHAPTER FOUR

Event 4 – "I am in a job which I do not like"

Points to Consider

1. Why am I in a job which I do not like? What value is it adding to me? How is it affecting me negatively?
2. What are the ways which can make this work more enjoyable and satisfactory? What actions I need to take?
3. What are my bigger goals? Is it helping me to get there? Which work would help me to get to my bigger goals?
4. How can I graduate from present job to the work of my liking, with least amount of risk?
5. How can I find people who can help me with this transition? How and when can I approach them for help?
6. What is my action plan?

CHAPTER FIVE

Event 5 – Failure in Exam

Points to Consider

1. What are the main reasons for my failure? Is it lack of interest or simply laziness? I need to understand that I am responsible for this event and I am the only person to correct it.
2. What this failure is indicating? Is it an indication that I am in a wrong field or something else? Which area I would be interested in where I would put my maximum efforts? How can I take actions for that?
3. Is it lack of work and sincerity, which has led to this failure? What are the reasons? How can I use this pain to direct my energies to work and success?
4. Who are my role models? What did they do to get success? What can I learn from them and decide my action plan?
5. What I need to be to get success? What actions I need to take immediately?

CHAPTER SIX

Event 6 – Poor Marks in Examination

Points to Consider

1. Who are the highest scorers in my examination? What are the main reasons for their excellent performance? How are they acting differently? What can I learn from them to get better marks?
2. Is it an indication that some correction is required in my actions? What are the reasons for low performance in examination? Is it interest or something else?
3. What am I interested in? What I need to do for it?
4. How do I need to change myself? What is my action plan?

CHAPTER SEVEN

Event 7 – Failure in Competitive Examination

Points to Consider

1. Do I really want to clear this competition? If yes, what learning & skills are missing in me?
2. What successful people have done rightly? What can I learn from them?
3. How can I build those skills? Who can guide and support me for this?
4. What actions I need to take? What is my action plan? What I need to do start taking action?
5. I need to set a limit of trying, after which I would leave it move on to other excellent opportunities. What is that limit? What are other great opportunities available to me?

CHAPTER EIGHT

Event 8 – Weak Performance at Work

Points to Consider

1. What are the main reasons for weak performance at work? Is it interest in work or lack of competencies?
2. If it is lack of interest in work, then what work would interest me? What I need to do to get it?
3. If it is lack of competencies, then what improvements are required? How can I get those competencies?
4. Who can guide and help me with this change or improvement? What actions I need to take?
5. What is my action plan? Take action.

CHAPTER NINE

Event 9 – Lack of Skills for a Job

Points to Consider

1. How and for what reasons I got this job? Why haven't I built these skills till now?
2. What skills I need to build and how can I learn those in shortest possible time?
3. Does my interest lie in doing this job or am I interested in something else?
4. What help and guidance I require and who can mentor me for that?
5. What I need to do for that? What is my action plan? Take action.

CHAPTER TEN

Event 10 - Broken Relationships

Points to Consider

1. Why this relation got broken up? How important this relation is for me?
2. What can I do to rebuild it? What correction I need to make in me?
3. Have I tried all possible options to work on this relationship? Am I satisfied with my efforts to save this relationship?
4. I cannot force the relationship on anyone. If it is not working, I should bow out of it respectfully without hurting or insulting anyone. I will let it go and move on.
5. What is my learning from this episode of my life? How would I implement this learning in my life?
6. What is next in my life? How can I make my existing relationships stronger and build new ones
7. How would I need to change myself? What actions I need to take?

CHAPTER ELEVEN

Event 11 – Cracks in Relationship

Points to Consider

1. Do I really like or love this person? Do I want to be in relation with him?
2. How is this relation to me? Is it emotional or based on mutual benefits?
3. What are the reasons for strain in relationship? Do I need to correct something?
4. I need to create more clarity and communication is the key for any solution. I need to have an honest conversation to rebuild this relation. My objective is to reestablish this relation, if it is not working out then we both should decently bow out of this relation.
5. What actions I need to take? Take action.

CHAPTER TWELVE

Event 12 – Missing Happiness from Life

Points to Consider

1. What are the reasons which are pushing me down? How can I come out of that?
2. What makes me happy? How should I indulge in those activities which make me happy?
3. Who are positive and mature people who can help me to come out of this mode? When should I meet them?
4. I need to completely disconnect from negative people? Who are negative people in my life? How can I be away from them?
5. Which are those activities where I can get small successes? When should I start doing those to get small successes?

CHAPTER THIRTEEN

Event 13 - Weak and Unfit Body

Points to Consider

1. How my body is giving me pain, restricting me and making me inefficient? How a great body would make be boundless to perform great tasks and live better?
2. What are the reasons which brought me here? What I need to do to leave them immediately?
3. What can I learn from the people with great body? Who can help and guide me in this quest?
4. What can I to do to start building a great body? What actions I need to take for getting the desired body shape?
5. How do I need to change myself for that? Which are the immediate changes?
6. What actions I need to take? What is my action plan? Take action.

CHAPTER FOURTEEN

Event 14 – Unsatisfactory Earning

Points to Consider

1. Why do I think that I am not able to earn enough? How is it affecting me and my material needs?
2. My happiness and satisfaction should not be affected by this deficiency. How can I make sure that anything is not affecting my love for life and happiness?
3. What can I do to improve my earnings consistently? Can I learn something from others who are earning well? What are my targets?
4. What changes I need to bring in me to get the required success? What actions I need to take to earn more than required?
5. What is my action plan? What actions I need to take immediately?

CHAPTER FIFTEEN

Event 15 – Failure in Business

Points to Consider

1. What are the main reasons for my failure in business? What should have I done for success in business? What is my learning?
2. What can I learn from others experiences for success in business? What new skills I need to develop to get success? What steps I need to take to develop the required skills?
3. What are the available opportunities in the market which I can exploit? What is my plan to monetize these opportunities?
4. I commit to do the right things to be a successful businessman.
5. How do I need to behave which would support me in building a robust business
6. What is my action plan? Which actions I need to take immediately?

CHAPTER SIXTEEN

Event 16 – Sluggish Business

Points to Consider

1. I need to keep trusting myself and my idea about its success. If it is not working which means that something needs to change. My goals are clear and I know what I need to do.
2. What are the reasons for this problem? What are my mistakes?
3. What different I need to do to strengthen my business? What can I learn from other successful players?
4. What actions I need to take for that? What is my action plan?
5. Take required action immediately.

CHAPTER SEVENTEEN

Event 17 – Trapped in Debt

Points to Consider

1. What are the reasons for me to get into this debt trap? What is my learning from this experience?
2. My immediate objective is to come out of this mess and commit to take every possible action, which is moral and legal, to repay it completely.
3. What are the different ways which can clear me of my debts? Which among these are best ones with least pain?
4. Which one I would like to execute and why? My main aim is to come out of debt and never get into it again.
5. What is my action plan? What actions I need to take immediately?
6. What is my learning from this experience? How would it improve my life in future?

CHAPTER EIGHTEEN

Event 18 – Feeling of Guilt

Points to Consider

1. What wrong I did? How someone suffered from my actions? What reasons were responsible for this action?
2. Can I neutralize those actions which caused suffering? Can I add some value to that person's life in some way? What actions I need to take for that?
3. How can I make sure that I would not repeat this action again in my life? What I need to do for that?
4. What I need to do to make sure that I never get involved in any action which causes guilt?
5. What is my action plan for above points?
6. I commit never to behave or act in a way which would lead to suffering to anyone.

CHAPTER NINETEEN

Event 19 – Bad Experiences

Points to Consider

1. I need to understand that my previous bad experiences are my past and none of my present actions are going to change that. The only thing which can change is my perception of these events.
2. What was the event and why I feel bad about it? How is this event still affecting me in wrong way?
3. Can I perceive it in a way that it empowers me? What can I learn from this event?
4. How can I improve myself by becoming stronger that similar things would never happen to me again?
5. What I need to be for becoming a person with right perceptions and actions?
6. What actions I need to take for achieving that aim?

CHAPTER TWENTY

Event 20 – Undesired Personality

Points to Consider

1. How would I define my personality? Why I consider it undesired?
2. What type of personality I appreciate? What personality I want to have?
3. Who can help me to achieve this improvement in my life? Do I need to take professional help?
4. How can I obliterate the undesired existing personality? What actions I need to take to become a person with desired personality?
5. What is my action plan? What actions I need to take immediately?
6. Take action?

CHAPTER TWENTY-ONE

Event 21 – Unattractive Looks

Points to Consider

1. How do I define unattractive looks? How do I fit in it?
2. How do I define a great person and how looks fit in it?
3. What I need to change in me to become a great person? What I need to become where looks would have minimum weightage?
4. What I need to do for that? What actions I need to take?
5. Commit for change and take action.

Event 22 – Bad Character

Points to Consider

1. What is a bad character? How do I fit in this definition?
2. What is a good character? Why I want it?
3. How can I change? What I need to leave? What I need to learn?
4. How can I do it? What actions I need to take for that?
5. Take action.

CHAPTER TWENTY-THREE

Event 23 – Addiction

Points to Consider

1. What is this addiction? Why is it wrong? How is it affecting me in a wrong way?
2. If it gives me pain then why am I not able to leave it? Why am I addicted to it?
3. How can I leave it with my commitment and will power?
4. Do I need to take some professional help to leave it?
5. What I need to do to leave this addiction?
6. What action I need to take?

CHAPTER TWENTY-FOUR

Event 24 – Unable to Work Hard

Points to Consider

1. How do I define hard work? Where do I rate myself on it? How is it affecting me negatively?
2. What is stopping me to work hard? Is it lack of interest or just laziness?
3. What activity is of my interest where I would put my maximum efforts?
4. I know the advantages and pleasure of peak performance and high productivity. I also understand the value it will add to my life.
5. How can I develop love for the work I do? What can I do for that? How can I be productive while working hard?
6. What actions I need to take?

CHAPTER TWENTY-FIVE

Event 25 – Poor Concentration

Points to Consider

1. What is my concentration level for the work I do? How do I rate it? How does it affect me?
2. How an improved concentration and focus would change my life? What value would it add?
3. What level of concentration I have during activities of my interest? What would lead to improve in concentration during other activities?
4. Can I learn something which can help me with enhancing concentration like meditation? Do I need to take help from some experts?
5. What I need to do? What is my action plan?

CHAPTER TWENTY-SIX

Event 26 – Jealousy

Points to Consider

1. What brings this feeling in me? Why? How is this feeling adding value to me or negatively affecting me?
2. Who is the only victim of this feeling? Can I divert my attention from it? Can I let it go?
3. Can I focus on something of my desire? What efforts are required from my side to get it?
4. How can I make sure that jealousy, of any type, does not exist in me?
5. What is my plan for action?

CHAPTER TWENTY-SEVEN

Event 27 – Hate for Others

Points to Consider

1. I understand that anger is my worst enemy as it always affects me negatively. Without anger I would be a more controlled and better person, who would have more happiness and success.
2. Whenever I am angry, I need to ask myself "Why am I hurting myself?"
3. I cannot give any person the power to control my emotions; anger gives the control of my emotions and actions to other person.
4. Anger is not going to solve any problem. Can I find the best way, logically, to solve the problem?
5. Forgiveness is the enemy of anger. If I can forgive, anger will vanish.
6. My focus and energies would be directed toward the activities I love and enjoy.
7. In future, I would be completely free of hateful feelings.

CHAPTER TWENTY-EIGHT

Event 28 – Not Loved Back

Points to Consider

1. Why do I feel that I am not loved back? I know that I cannot force anyone to love me. I need to be a just and moral person, who is genuine and can be relied.
2. I need to be satisfied and happy with myself. I need to keep learning and improving.
3. I would believe in giving and helping others without expecting anything in return.
4. I would commit to live a principled life. I would be loved back.
5. What I need to be to change myself? What I need to do?
6. What is my action plan? What actions I need to take immediately?

CHAPTER TWENTY-NINE

Event 29 – Influence of Bad Beliefs

Points to Consider

1. Why are these beliefs bad? What negative effect they have on me? How have these beliefs restricted me from growth and happiness?
2. What are my bad beliefs? For each belief, raise questions about proving the belief wrong. Why this belief has no basis? Which are the real life cases proving this belief wrong?
3. Find good empowering beliefs. Replace bad ones with these empowering beliefs. Reinforce them repeatedly.
4. I need to be in the company of people with right beliefs and stop interaction with people with wrong beliefs.
5. What actions I need to take immediately?

CHAPTER THIRTY

Event 30 – Unsurpassable Barrier

Points to Consider

1. What is the barrier which is blocking my progress? Is it internal, in my mind or external set by a system or person? What are the reasons that I am not able to cross it?
2. How is it affecting me negatively? What is required to cross it? Who is able to cross it successfully? What can I learn from these successful people about crossing the barrier?
3. What benefits will I get if I cross this barrier? What opportunities will I miss if I do not cross this barrier?
4. What I need to do to cross or break it? What resource do I require? How would I arrange for these resources?
5. What changes are required in me to break this barrier? How can I bring those changes?
6. What is my action plan? What actions I need to take?

Event 31 – Lack of Desired Results

Points to Consider

1. I am working hard but I am not able to get the desired results.
2. Am I working right, by putting the required honest efforts? Are my efforts directed in the right direction? Am I working hard and smartly? What can I learn from successful people who are able to get desired results?
3. What I need to do to get the desired results? What more is required for it, in terms of efforts and resources? What need to change in me?
4. What is my action plan? What action I need to take immediately?

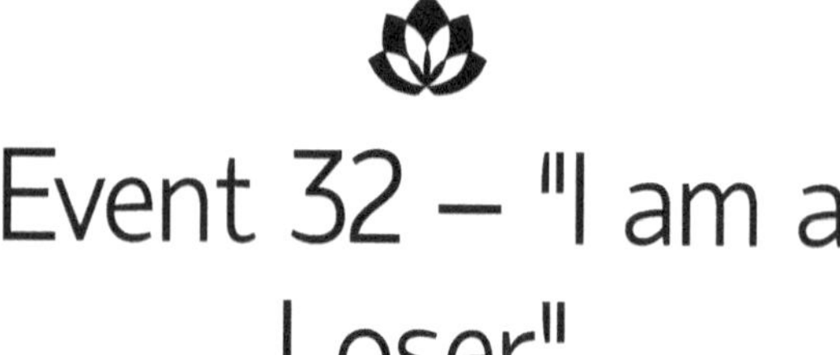

Event 32 – "I am a Loser"

Points to Consider

1. Who considers me a loser? Why? What do I feel about myself? Why?
2. Who are winners? How are they different from me?
3. How can I be a winner? What I need to achieve & how I need to behave for that?
4. How would my life change when I am a winner?
5. How I need to change for being a winner?
6. What actions I need to take?

CHAPTER THIRTY-THREE

Event 33 – Peer Pressure

Points to Consider

1. Why I consider others doing better than me? How am I doing in comparison to them? Why are they doing better than me? What is my learning?
2. What is the definition of success for me? How I rate myself on that?
3. From now onwards my focus would be on setting and meeting goals which would lead me to success.
4. How I need to change myself for getting success? What I need to learn?
5. What actions I need to take?

CHAPTER THIRTY-FOUR

Event 34 – Devoid of Luxury

Points to Consider

1. Why I want luxurious things? How they add value to me?
2. How can I improve my earnings to be able to afford luxury?
3. What I need to learn to be able to earn more? How I need to change?
4. What I need to be to achieve luxury? I will always be ethical and moral.
5. What is my action plan? What actions I need to take immediately?

CHAPTER THIRTY-FIVE

Event 35 – Death

Points to Consider

1. What can I do to ease my pain of loss? Can I contribute to improve lives of people and ease other's pain?
2. As that person is no more with me what can I do now? How would he feel to see me in pain?
3. What should I do to keep his legacy alive and make people remember him as a great person?
4. He would remain with me forever, what should I do in my life which would make him proud?
5. How should I live my life so that I have no regrets in my death?

CHAPTER THIRTY-SIX

Event 36 – Handicap

Points to Consider

1. Now that this is a fact of my life, how can I use the opportunities available to me for making my life successful and generous?
2. What I need to do to minimize the effects of my handicap in my daily tasks? Can any equipment or technology help me?
3. My family and friends feel sad for me, I need to remain brave and motivated to give them happiness. My enthusiasm for life is the key to everyone's happiness.
4. Can this be an opportunity for me? Can I do something now which I couldn't do when I was normal, which would give me happiness faster?
5. I would find and meet the winners whose spirits were not dampened even after getting handicapped.
6. What actions I need to take?

CHAPTER THIRTY-SEVEN

Event 37- Monitory Loss

Points to Consider

1. What wrong I did that the money was lost? What winners did differently?
2. I am richer with experience. I would be wealthier (with experience) if I could come out of this loss, stronger. What I need to do for that?
3. What is my learning with this experience? How can I use it to become a winner and get more than I lost?
4. What should be my next steps? What action I need to take? What is my action plan?
5. Take action.

CHAPTER THIRTY-EIGHT

Event 38 – Deceived

Points to Consider

1. How was I deceived? What wrong I did?
2. What were the indications I missed, which pointed towards the reality of the person?
3. What is my learning from this event? How will I be careful next time?
4. How would I make sure that I do not have any negativity or hate? This event will not make me to stop trusting people, but I would be careful, next time, while trusting people.
5. This experience is enough to teach me that I should not break anyone's trust on me.

CHAPTER THIRTY-NINE

Event 39 – Slow Learner

Points to Consider

1. What are the main reasons of my slow speed of learning? Is it interest or something else?
2. What other successful learners are doing different than me? What can I learn from them?
3. Can I take guidance and support from experts and teachers who can help me to bridge the gap? Who are those people? How should I approach them?
4. What corrections I need to make in me to be a better learner? I am committed for it and ready to do take any action for that.
5. What is my action plan? Take action.

CHAPTER FORTY

Event 40 – Repeating the Mistakes

Points to Consider

1. What mistakes am I repeating? What are the reasons for that?
2. Why am I inflicting pain on me, repeatedly? Is it carelessness or habit or something else?
3. What actions I need to take to stop this habit? Who can help me in this?
4. What is my action plan?
5. Take action.
6. I will keep working on this process till this habit is nonexistent.

CHAPTER FORTY-ONE

Event 41 – Not Able to Get Success

Points to Consider

1. The formula of success is opportunity meeting the right preparation. Am I doing this right?
2. Who are the successful people, what can I learn from their actions?
3. Is it possible that my efforts are not enough and I need to put more efforts? What changes are required in me to get success?
4. What I need to do to get these changes? I would keep learning from every failure till I do just right.
5. I would commit to perseverance till I get success.

CHAPTER FORTY-TWO

Event 42 – Alone

Points to Consider

1. What are the reasons for me being alone? Why I am not connecting with others? Is it behavior or wrong beliefs or something else? What I need to do to correct myself?
2. If I decide that I will not be alone, what actions will I need to take?
3. Who are those people with whom I can connect immediately? When would I connect with these people?
4. What I need to do to get into a relationship? What all places can I visit where I can connect with people?
5. The connection with people will never be at the cost of my self-respect and self-esteem.

Event 43 – Poverty

Points to Consider

1. Why am I poor? What reasons have let me to this level? What successful people are doing rightly? What can I learn from them?
2. How can I make myself better? What skills and competencies do I need to have?
3. What I need to be to earn reputation and respect? What is the area in which I can be best? What I need to do to be best in the chosen area?
4. I would be sincere for my work. I have clarity about my purpose, vision and goals. I am committed to achieve them. My actions will always be ethical and moral. I have clarity about my principles of life.
5. As I have much less to lose, I can take risks. What business can I start? What I need to do to be a business owner? I am not going to stop till I get to my target, however long it may take.
6. What can I do to help others? How can I build a team of like-minded people who would work with me to get success?

CHAPTER FORTY-FOUR

Event 44 – Living in a Poor Country

Points to Consider

1. Who are the successful people? What are they doing rightly? What can I learn from them?
2. What are the opportunities available now for me? What I need to do to monetize them?
3. What I need to learn? How I need to change to get success? Can someone guide and support me in this endeavor?
4. What can I learn from successful business models in developed countries? How can I customize those models for my country? How can these business models would be opportunities for me?
5. What I need to be to get success in this country? I will work hard, smartly.
6. What is my action plan? What actions I need to take immediately?

CHAPTER FORTY-FIVE

Event 45 - Fear of Something

Points to Consider

1. What do I Fear? What are the reasons for it? How others got success with similar fear? What can I learn from them?
2. I need to face my fear, safely. How can I prepare myself to face this fear? What I need to do to face this fear? Do I need to take some professional help?
3. I will keep facing this fear till it loses its strength on me.
4. What I need to learn? How I have to change myself?
5. What actions I need to take?

CHAPTER FORTY-SIX

Event 46 – Lost Something You Love

Points to Consider

1. How was it lost? Can I do something about it now? If not, I will remember it beautifully.
2. How can I involve myself into something which gives me enthusiasm and motivation?
3. How can I involve myself into meditation and activities to help others?
4. Which activities would add value to me and the people I love? What I need to do for that?
5. How can I change myself for being a better person?
6. What actions I need to take?

CHAPTER FORTY-SEVEN

Event 47 – Desire for a Normal Life

Points to Consider

1. Why am I considering my life as tough? What routine I consider as normal? What is stopping me to get that routine?
2. Do I know people who are living an ideal life? What right are they doing? What decision they took to get this life?
3. What changes are required in me to get the desired life and routine? What decisions I need to take? What I need to commit?
4. What is my action plan? What actions I need to take now?

CHAPTER FORTY-EIGHT

Event 48 – Unlucky

Points to Consider

1. Why I consider myself unlucky? Why I perceive it this way?
2. All happenings in my life are the choices I made and decisions I took. If I could choose better options and take better decisions then I would get better results. What I need to do to improve my choices and decisions?
3. How other positive and successful people behave and act? What can I learn?
4. How can I change my perception to positive, which would look for opportunities and brighter side of life? How would it change my life?
5. What I need to do to perceive all challenging situations as positive and use them to add value to me? What should be the required principles of my life to which I can commit to?
6. What I need to be to become that "Lucky" person? What actions I need to take?

CHAPTER FORTY-NINE

Event 49 – No Peace of Mind

Points to Consider

1. Why I do not have the peace of mind? What could be the reasons for this chaos?
2. What wrong I am doing which is putting my mind in chaos? What actions would neutralize chaos in my mind and make my mind peaceful? What value the peace of mind would add in my life?
3. Who are the people with complete peace of mind? What right are they doing? What can I learn from them?
4. What principles are required in my life to which I need to commit to? What I need to be to get the desired peace of mind?
5. What is my action plan? What I need to do?

CHAPTER FIFTY

Event 50 – I am Hated

Points to Consider

1. Why do I say that I am hated by others? What are the reasons that they hate me? What am I doing wrong?
2. Who are loved and liked by others? Why are they loved by people? What can I learn from them?
3. What I need to change in me? What thinking, behavior and actions which need to disappear and what are the principles I need to commit? What new things I need to learn?
4. Can I take help from a trusted person? What I need to be to earn the trust of people?
5. What is my plan of action? What actions I need to take?

CHAPTER FIFTY-ONE

Event 51 – I Dislike Climate

Points to Consider

1. Why I do not like the climate? How is it creating problems for me? Can I do anything to change the climate? If not, I need to accept this fact and try to enjoy it while getting success in this climate.
2. Can I leave this place and shift to a place with nice climate? I need to take a decision.
3. How other positive people enjoy the place and climate? What can I learn from them? What I need to do to be in touch with positive people who can bring positivity in my life?
4. How can I enjoy this climate? What fun activities are available? How can I shift my negative thinking to constructive?
5. What needs to be done to be away from negative personalities who spreads passiveness?
6. What is my plan of action? What actions I need to take immediately?

CHAPTER FIFTY-TWO

Event 52 – Monday Blues

Points to Consider

1. Why I hate Monday mornings? Is there someone who enjoys Mondays? Is there something which I can learn from them?
2. It happens when my life is not properly balanced or in do not like my work. What are the reasons contributing to Monday Blues? What is missing which is leading me to dissatisfaction? What can I do to fix it? What should happen to make my Mondays enjoyable?
3. How do I need to change for that? What decisions I need to take?
4. What actions I need to take?

CHAPTER FIFTY-THREE

Event 53 – Long Days and Weeks

Points to Consider

1. Why I consider my work days and weeks as long? How are these affecting me mentally, physically and emotionally? What would be the right thing which should happen to optimize everything in life? How can I make sure that it happens?
2. Who is having optimized days and weeks, which let them enjoy life? How are they able to do it? What can I learn?
3. What is wrong in my plans and actions? What should change? What is the right thing to do? What decisions I need to take?
4. What I need to do? What is my action plan?

CHAPTER FIFTY-FOUR

Event 54 – Unbalanced Personal and Professional Life

Points to Consider

1. Why I say it unbalanced? Why is this happening? How is it affecting me?
2. I understand that both personal and professional lives are important to me and I must have the right balance to live a fulfilled life.
3. Logically, what is the right amount of weight which should be allotted to both, to give me fulfillment? What I need to do to get this balance in life?
4. Where I am wrong? What are the corrections I need to make in my decisions and actions?
5. What can I learn from those people who are managing it well? How do I need to change myself? What do I need to do to get the right balance?
6. What is my plan of action?

CHAPTER FIFTY-FIVE

Event 55 – No Options

Points to Consider

1. Why am I saying that I have no options? What can be the reasons for this thinking? What wrong am I thinking and doing which is drying up options for me? Am I missing some areas and options which I have not considered?
2. How would my life change if I am able to create or get several options in my life? How would it help me to get success?
3. Who are the people which have enough options in their life? How are they able to get options? What is right in their thinking and actions? What can I learn from them?
4. How do I need to change my thinking and action? What more I need to try?
5. What do I need to do? What is my plan of action?

CHAPTER FIFTY-SIX

Event 56 – No Opportunities

Points to Consider

1. Why do I say this? What are the reasons of not finding opportunities in my life? How is it affecting my growth? Did I miss any area where I can find opportunities?
2. How would my life become better if I am able to get opportunities? What value these opportunities would add to my life?
3. For whom the opportunities are available in plenty? How are they able to get opportunities? What is right in their decisions and actions? What is my learning? What is the gap which I need to fill?
4. What changes are required in me? What I need to do to bring those changes in me?
5. I need to remain motivated, committed and optimistic about opportunities in my life. I understand that availability of options is not enough; I should be able to utilize these opportunities to get success. What skills and thought-process is required to take the full benefits

of available opportunities?

6. What is my action plan? What actions I need to take immediately?

CHAPTER FIFTY-SEVEN

Event 57 – Accident

Points to Consider

1. What is my loss with accident? What is my learning?
2. How can I recover from physical, mental and emotional injuries? What is required to be done? Do I need to take professional help to recover fast?
3. I understand that this is a fact and I need to come out of the trauma of accident. I need to look at the positive side of life and make the best out of it. What are the opportunities with me, which would help me to get success?
4. What are the opportunities which are open for me now? How can I take the best use of my skills? What I need to learn? What decisions I need to take?
5. How do I need to change myself for getting best possible results?
6. What is required to be done now? What is my action plan?

Event 58 - Lack of Excitement

Points to Consider

1. Why do I lack excitement in life? What activities make me enthusiastic? Why these activities are missing from my life?
2. What is my purpose of life for which I am committed and emotionally connected? How my purpose would help me to set personal and professional goals? What I need to do for setting goals?
3. What skills and competencies I need to gain? What I need to do for that?
4. What changes are required in me?
5. What is my action plan? What actions I need to take?

CHAPTER FIFTY-NINE

Event 59 – No Time for Myself

Points to Consider

1. I understand that time is limited and I need to manage my time for activities I love.
2. What is keeping me busy? What is unimportant work? What is my priority of work?
3. How can I improve my productivity and time management to get more time for myself? What decisions I need to take?
4. How task masters are able to manage work and interest simultaneously? What can I learn from them?
5. What are the activities of my interest? How can I include these activities in my life? What changes are required in me?
6. What is my new schedule of work, which is efficient, effective and includes activities on my interest? I need to commit to execute it.
7. What actions I need to take?

CHAPTER SIXTY

Event 60 – Others Control Me

Points to Consider

1. It is my choice that I let other control my life. I have to just choose to take control of my destiny back from others, in my own hands.
2. Why am I letting others to control my life? How has this started? How is it affecting me? How is it restricting me to achieve my potential and get happiness?
3. What can I learn from those successful people who control their decisions and actions?
4. How can I come out of this framework without affecting my normal life? What I need to do for that?
5. What I want to be in my life? What is my ambition? What is my next target?
6. What should change in me? What decisions I need to take? How can I execute those decisions?
7. What is my action plan? What actions I need to take immediately?

CHAPTER SIXTY-ONE

Event 61 – Luckless

Points to Consider

1. I understand that luck is opportunity meeting preparations. I could not take advantage of previous opportunities because my mistakes, which should be remedied. I need to take actions to get ready to take advantages of the opportunities available.
2. Why do I consider myself luckless? What opportunities did I miss and what were the reasons for that? What would have allowed me to take advantage of these opportunities? What changes are required in me?
3. What can I learn from winners who are always lucky as they control their luck? What is the gap which I need to fill?
4. What I need to do to be better at thinking, decision making and actions?
5. What I need to be to control my own luck? What I need to learn? How can I improve my competencies and skills set?
6. What is my action plan? What actions I need to take immediately?

CHAPTER SIXTY-TWO

Event 62 – Hopelessness

Points to Consider

1. Why do I have hopelessness in life? What are the reasons for that? How is it affecting me? How my life would change if I become more optimistic?
2. Who have optimism and excitement in life? Why they have that? How are they different from me? What can I learn from them?
3. What are my dreams, what I want to be? What I need to do to get those dreams? What I need to learn?
4. What changes are required in me? What I need to do?
5. What actions do I need to take?

CHAPTER SIXTY-THREE

Event 63 – Not Responsible

Points to Consider

1. Why am I not able to meet my goals? Why am I not responsible? How does it affect me? How my life would change if I am able to meet my goals and I become more responsible?
2. What can I learn from winners who are responsible and meet their goals? How are they able to do it? What is their thinking process and how they act?
3. I need to set goals which can be met and take responsibilities which I can fulfill. I need to be completely sincere to meet them. What are my short term and long term goals? What I need to do to meet them?
4. How can I take more initiations and responsibilities? How can I make sure that I meet them? Can someone help or guide me to become a better person?
5. What actions I need to take?

CHAPTER SIXTY-FOUR

Event 64 – Resolutions Not Kept

Points to Consider

1. Why am I not able to keep the resolutions? What wrong am I doing? How my resolution would help me in my life? What are the reasons I am not able to commit to it?
2. Who gets success with their resolutions? What different are they doing? What can I learn from them?
3. How do I need to change myself to keep my resolutions? What principles I need to commit?
4. I understand the nothing but my will-power and commitment would help me to keep my resolutions.
5. What actions I need to take immediately?

CHAPTER SIXTY-FIVE

Event 65 – Do Not Feel Happy in Life

Points to Consider

1. How do I define happiness? Why I do not feel it? What wrong have I done that I do not have it? What can give me happiness?
2. How happy people are different than me? What is their thinking process? What is my learning from them?
3. How my thinking process should change to make me a happy person? What I need to do to get that thinking process? What I should never do?
4. What principles I need to follow strictly? What commitments I need to make?
5. What is my action plan? Which actions I need to take immediately?

CHAPTER SIXTY-SIX

Event 66 – "I Should Have"

Points to Consider

1. "I should have" is a tool for regret, which makes me feel miserable. "I should have done that", "I should have not spoken that" etc. would focus on the past to make me glum.
2. "I should have" should be replaced by "I have" and "I would".
3. Why I keep saying "I should have"? How does it affect me? How can I focus on practical activities which can add value to me?
4. I need to commit to never regret for the past events, instead learn from them to improve my decisions.
5. How can my decisions and actions improve, so that I never have to regret?

CHAPTER SIXTY-SEVEN

Event 67 – Laziness

Points to Consider

1. Why do I call myself lazy? How is it affecting me? What pain do I get from this habit?
2. What are the reasons for laziness? Is it interest or lack of focus?
3. How am I different from dynamic and active people? How they are able keep themselves energetic? What can I learn from them?
4. What activities can bring enthusiasm in my life? What I need to do get those activities in my daily routine?
5. What are the keys to active life to which I can commit?
6. What is my action plan? What actions I need to take?

CHAPTER SIXTY-EIGHT

Event 68 - No Connection with God

Points to Consider

1. How do I define God? Do I believe in God or some higher powers? How would my life become better with belief?
2. What unique I have seen in people with belief in God? Why do I want to be like them? What their actions teach me?
3. Can I speak to someone I trust, who can guide and explain me the concept? What changes are required in me? What actions I need to take to bring that change?
4. How my daily routine would change? What commitments I need to make?
5. What is my action plan?

Event 69 – Punished by God

Points to Consider

1. Why do I consider myself punished by God? What are the reasons?
2. I need to stop blaming God for every wrong in my life and start looking at my thinking, behavior and actions which are not letting me get success?
3. Who are successful and happy people? What can I learn from them about better thinking process, behavior and actions?
4. What I need to be to be a better person? What changes are required in me? What principles should I commit to?
5. What actions do I need to take?

Event 70 – Not an Achiever

Points to Consider

1. Why do I say this about me? What are my experiences? What results I could not get? What are the reasons for failure? What actions were required?
2. How winning would change my life?
3. How the achievers behave and act? What is their thinking process? What can I learn from them?
4. What needs to change in me? What I need to do to build those abilities? What skill-set I need to build?
5. What is my action plan? What actions I need to take?

CHAPTER SEVENTY-ONE

Event 71 - I Want to be Genuine

Points to Consider

1. How am I perceived now? Why I am not considered as genuine? What wrong I do – habit, behavior or actions?
2. What I need to change in me that would build me into a genuine person?
3. What principles would I need to follow?
4. What are those activities which I will never do?
5. What action I need to take now to be on that path?

CHAPTER SEVENTY-TWO

Event 72 - I Want to be Trusted

Points to Consider

1. Do I understand the responsibility associated with people trusting me? Am I serious about it?
2. What do I feel about the people I trust? How are they different? Why people trust them? What can I learn from them?
3. How can I change my behavior and actions to a person who is honest, has life principles, is genuine and can be trusted?
4. Take small responsibilities and build trust. With time build it stronger.
5. What actions would break trust? How can I improve my thinking process where right actions become a natural part of me?
6. To which principles should I commit?
7. What actions I need to take?

CHAPTER SEVENTY-THREE

Event 73 – I Hide Many Secrets

Points to Consider

1. What am I hiding? How does it affect me and others?
2. Why do I have guilt feeling with this? What needs to be done to have better empowering feelings?
3. What actions I should take? How my actions would harm me and others? What should be done?
4. How can I make sure that I never get into similar situation? What commitments I need to make?
5. What is my action plan?

About Author

Anshuman is an author and knowledge creator who has transformed the lives and work of people from every continent. His groundbreaking ideas in Thinking, Communication, Personality and Storytelling are revolutionary, simple and effective.

His belief in simplicity has created powerful solutions that can be used by everyone effortlessly.

Experience the free material from following links:

https://direct.me/anshuman

www.ingramcontent.com/pod-product-compliance
Lightning Source LLC
Chambersburg PA
CBHW031456150726
47990CB00007B/2778